CHILDREN JUST LIKE ME

HOW TO USE THIS BOOK

Read about the daily lives of children from around the world, then decorate the pages with the colorful stickers from the center of this booklet. Choose the sticker that best matches the caption description and fits the space available. Then match the flag stickers to the right countries on the continent maps.

> Put a
> photograph of
> yourself in
> this space.

This is me

A DK PUBLISHING BOOK

First American Edition, 1998

4 6 8 10 9 7 5

Published in the United States by
DK Publishing, Inc.
95 Madison Avenue
New York, New York 10016

Visit us on the World Wide Web at http://www.dk.com

Published in Great Britain by Dorling Kindersley Limited.

ISBN 0-7894-3626-4

Reproduced by Colourscan, Singapore
Printed and bound by Graphicom, Italy

The Americas

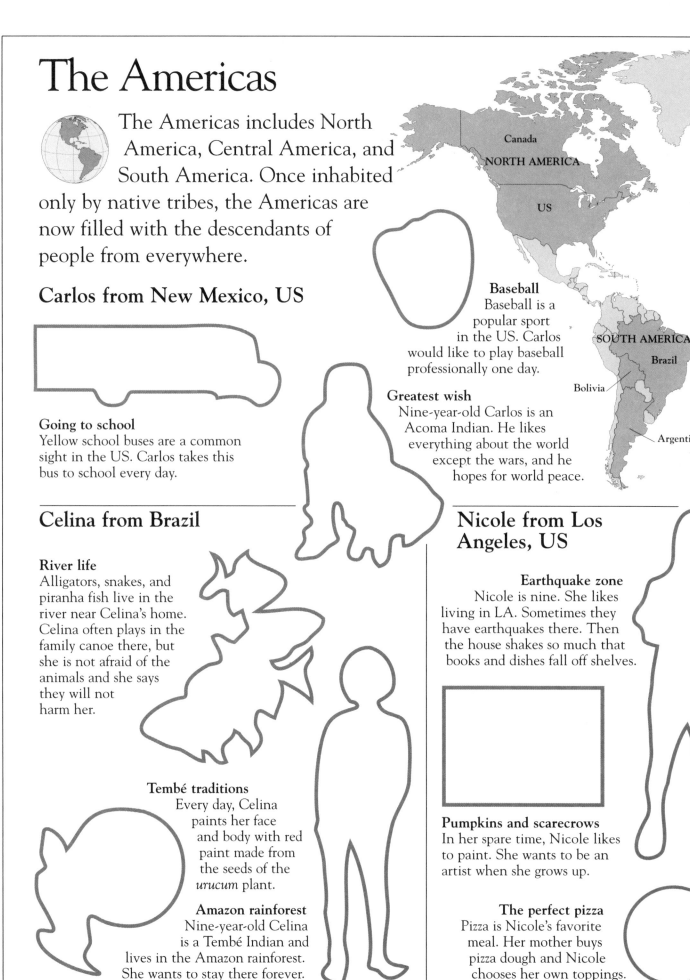

The Americas includes North America, Central America, and South America. Once inhabited only by native tribes, the Americas are now filled with the descendants of people from everywhere.

Carlos from New Mexico, US

Going to school
Yellow school buses are a common sight in the US. Carlos takes this bus to school every day.

Baseball
Baseball is a popular sport in the US. Carlos would like to play baseball professionally one day.

Greatest wish
Nine-year-old Carlos is an Acoma Indian. He likes everything about the world except the wars, and he hopes for world peace.

Celina from Brazil

River life
Alligators, snakes, and piranha fish live in the river near Celina's home. Celina often plays in the family canoe there, but she is not afraid of the animals and she says they will not harm her.

Tembé traditions
Every day, Celina paints her face and body with red paint made from the seeds of the *urucum* plant.

Amazon rainforest
Nine-year-old Celina is a Tembé Indian and lives in the Amazon rainforest. She wants to stay there forever.

Nicole from Los Angeles, US

Earthquake zone
Nicole is nine. She likes living in LA. Sometimes they have earthquakes there. Then the house shakes so much that books and dishes fall off shelves.

Pumpkins and scarecrows
In her spare time, Nicole likes to paint. She wants to be an artist when she grows up.

The perfect pizza
Pizza is Nicole's favorite meal. Her mother buys pizza dough and Nicole chooses her own toppings.

Map labels: Canada, NORTH AMERICA, US, SOUTH AMERICA, Brazil, Bolivia, Argentina

Oscar from Bolivia

Crazy about soccer
Oscar loves to play soccer. When he grows up he wants to be a professional.

High in the mountains
Nine-year-old Oscar is an Aymara Indian. He lives on a farm far up in the Andean mountains, by Lake Titicaca.

Mealtime
Oscar often eats noodle soup with rice and potatoes. He likes to help collect the potatoes from the fields.

Levi from Canada

Baffin Island
Eight-year-old Levi and his sister Naiomi are *Inuk* (Inuit), a native people of northern Canada. They live on the cold, arctic coast of Baffin Island, where it snows for about eight months each year.

Caribou
Throughout the year, herds of wild reindeer, called caribou, roam Baffin Island.

Ice-hockey toy
In his spare time, Levi likes playing ice hockey. He supports his local team, called the Atoms.

Carlitos from Argentina

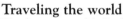

Traveling the world
Twelve-year-old Carlitos lives on a cattle ranch. His given name is Carlos, but everyone calls him Carlitos. When he grows up he would like to travel around the world.

Mate tea
Mate is a popular Argentinian drink. Carlitos drinks *mate* for breakfast and when friends come to visit. He drinks it through a special straw to strain out the leaves.

Life on the ranch
Horses are a common sight on the ranch. Carlitos likes to help round up the cattle on horseback. He rides his horse as close to the cattle as he can, then calls to them so that they run the right way.

Car racing
Carlitos likes playing games with his toy race car.

Europe

Europe stretches from the northern arctic coasts of Russia to the warm Mediterranean countries in the south. Many Europeans live in busy, crowded towns and cities.

Rachel from France

Feline friends
Cats are Rachel's favorite animals. Her bedroom walls are covered with cat posters.

Rock singer
Rachel is nine and lives in a french castle, called a château. She loves rock and jazz music and would like to be a singer.

Family treasure
This doll once belonged to Rachel's great-grandmother. It is Rachel's favorite toy.

Olia from Russia

Christmas presents
Father Frost gives kids presents on January first. Olia was given this toy dog.

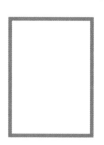

Picture perfect
Olia likes painting. She copied this picture from a book of fairytales.

Ballet dancer
Eight-year-old Olia's given name is Olga. She lives near Moscow, the capital of Russia and is training to be a ballet dancer at the Russian Classical Dance School.

Ari from Finland

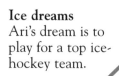

Salmon fishing
Ari loves fishing. He would fish every day if he could.

Ice dreams
Ari's dream is to play for a top ice-hockey team.

Two languages
Eleven-year-old Ari lives in the far north of Finland. His family belongs to the Saame people and Ari can speak both Saame and Finnish.

Bogna from Poland

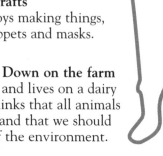

Arts and crafts
Bogna enjoys making things, such as puppets and masks.

Down on the farm
Bogna is ten and lives on a dairy farm. She thinks that all animals are precious and that we should take care of the environment.

EVERYDAY THINGS

Pumpkin-field drawing

Toy race car

Doll

Body paint

Toy helicopter

Soccer ball

Paper mask

Dinosaur drawing

Fairytale painting

Football drawing

Butterfly drawing

Puppet and mask

Strawberries

Ice-hockey toy

Pizza

Fruits

Toy dog

Ice-hockey stick and skates

Ankle bracelets

Basketball

Festival kites

Cat

Baseball glove and ball

Ranch horse

Maasai bead necklace

Jae gi tinsel ball

Duck drawing

CHILDREN OF THE WORLD

Rachel

Ngawaiata

Celina

Edgar

Carlitos

Olia

Guo
Shuang

Oscar

Thi Liên

Subaedah

Levi and Naiomi

Suchart

Ghana

Egypt

Canada

Tanzania

Poland

Thailand

Finland

Bolivia

Brazil

Argentina

South Korea

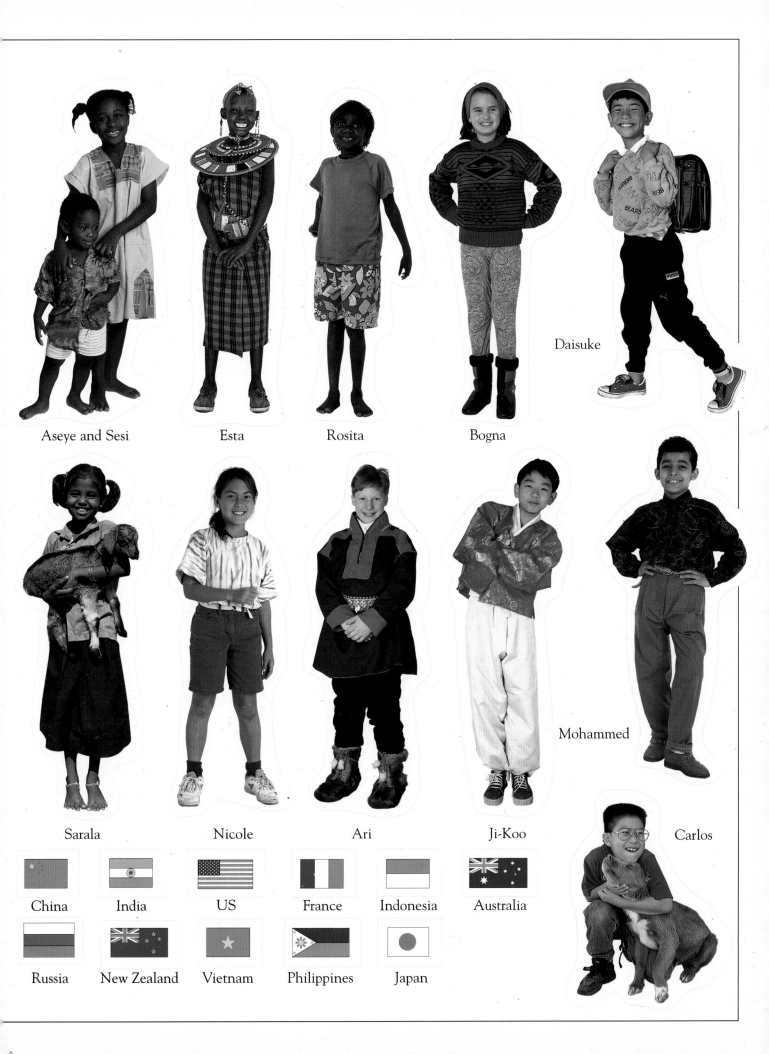

Aseye and Sesi

Esta

Rosita

Bogna

Daisuke

Sarala

Nicole

Ari

Ji-Koo

Mohammed

Carlos

China

India

US

France

Indonesia

Australia

Russia

New Zealand

Vietnam

Philippines

Japan

DAILY LIFE

African elephant

Bowl of rice

Temple offerings

Piranha fish

Gabiny fruits

Noodle soup

Hibiscus flower

Noodle dish

Mate tea

Dolphins

Salmon

Caribou

Meat dumplings

Bougainvillea plant

African lion

Plantains and mixed vegetables

Clay vase

Papaya fruits

Rice cakes

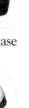

Oysters

School bus

Clown fish

Pumpkin

Africa

The African landscape ranges from vast deserts to steamy rainforests, from open, grassy plains to mountain ranges. There are large cities, but many people still live in the countryside, called "the bush."

Egypt

Ghana

Tanzania

Mohammed from Egypt

Favorite food
Mohammed loves eating strawberries.

Soccer fan
This soccer ball was given to Mohammed by his father. It is his most treasured possession.

Life in the city
Nine-year-old Mohammed likes living in Cairo, but he thinks there is too much traffic there. He wants to be a policeman when he's older.

Esta from Tanzania

Fun and games
Twelve-year-old Esta likes to play with the toys that she makes out of the clay soil. She also likes to play catch with her friends.

Bead jewelry
All Maasai women wear necklaces like these. Esta's necklace is made from lots of tiny beads.

Local wildlife
The lions that live in the countryside nearby scare Esta, although she has never seen one.

Aseye from Ghana

Plantains for dinner
Aesye eats lots of fried and boiled plantains and mixed vegetables.

School lessons
Seven-year-old Aseye lives in Accra, Ghana's capital. She likes learning about biology at school and wants to be a doctor when she grows up.

Too big
Elephants frighten Aseye. They are so big that she is worried they might step on her and squash her.

Asia

Asia is the world's largest continent. Over two-thirds of the world's population live here, especially in the southern and eastern regions.

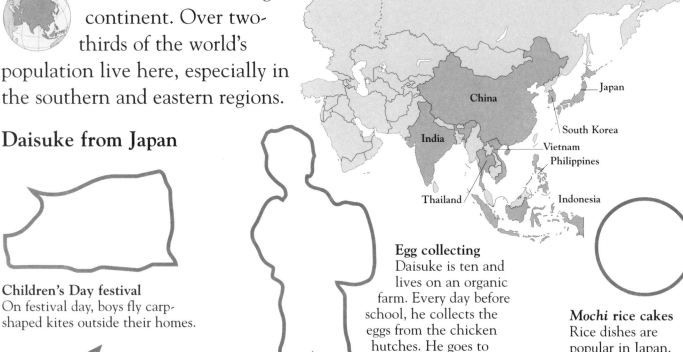

China
Japan
India
South Korea
Vietnam
Philippines
Thailand
Indonesia

Daisuke from Japan

Children's Day festival
On festival day, boys fly carp-shaped kites outside their homes.

Dinosaurs
Daisuke loves dinosaurs and wants to study dinosaur fossils when he grows up.

Egg collecting
Daisuke is ten and lives on an organic farm. Every day before school, he collects the eggs from the chicken hutches. He goes to school six days a week.

Mochi rice cakes
Rice dishes are popular in Japan. These rice cakes are wrapped in seaweed.

Suchart from Thailand

Temple offerings
Early each morning, Suchart and the other novice monks visit the village to collect temple offerings of food, candles, and flowers.

Fruit trees
Papaya fruits grow wild on the trees around Suchart's temple.

Buddhist monk
Suchart is twelve. He lives in a temple and is studying to be a Buddhist monk. He likes to play soccer with the other novices.

Guo Shuang from China

Dinner time
For supper, Guo Shuang's mother often makes meat dumplings with garlic and ginger.

Favorite pastimes
Nine-year-old Guo Shuang lives near Beijing, the capital of China. She loves reading and watching cartoons on TV.

Handicrafts
Guo Shuang loves to make things, like this mask. She wants to teach crafts when she is older.

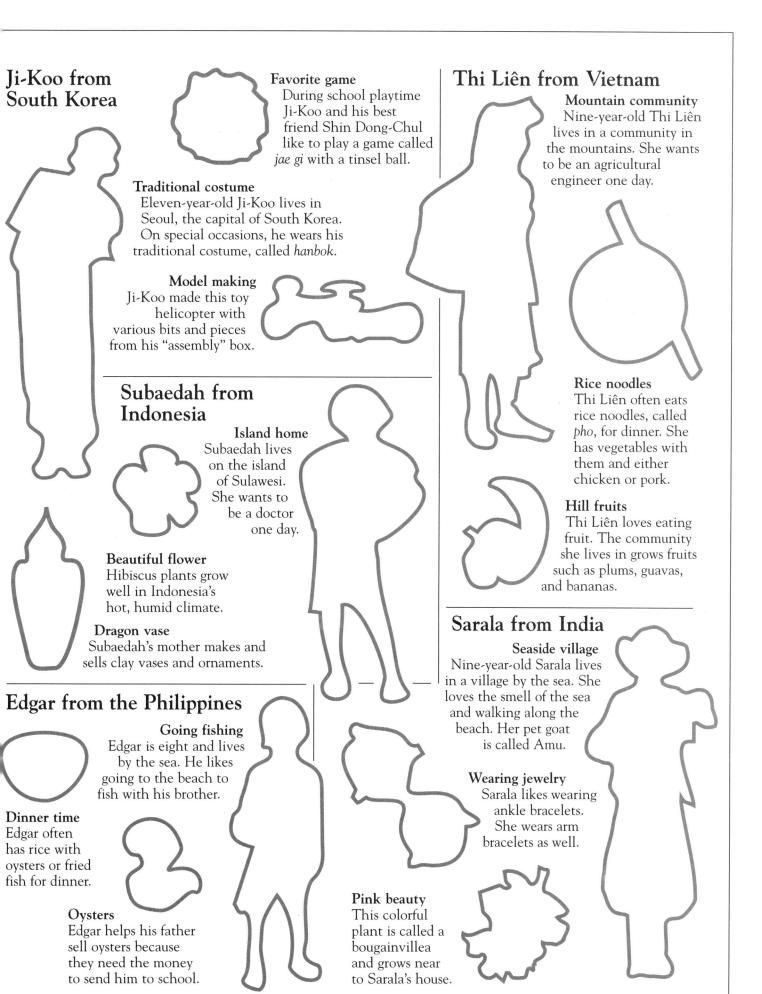

Ji-Koo from South Korea

Favorite game
During school playtime Ji-Koo and his best friend Shin Dong-Chul like to play a game called *jae gi* with a tinsel ball.

Traditional costume
Eleven-year-old Ji-Koo lives in Seoul, the capital of South Korea. On special occasions, he wears his traditional costume, called *hanbok*.

Model making
Ji-Koo made this toy helicopter with various bits and pieces from his "assembly" box.

Subaedah from Indonesia

Island home
Subaedah lives on the island of Sulawesi. She wants to be a doctor one day.

Beautiful flower
Hibiscus plants grow well in Indonesia's hot, humid climate.

Dragon vase
Subaedah's mother makes and sells clay vases and ornaments.

Edgar from the Philippines

Going fishing
Edgar is eight and lives by the sea. He likes going to the beach to fish with his brother.

Dinner time
Edgar often has rice with oysters or fried fish for dinner.

Oysters
Edgar helps his father sell oysters because they need the money to send him to school.

Thi Liên from Vietnam

Mountain community
Nine-year-old Thi Liên lives in a community in the mountains. She wants to be an agricultural engineer one day.

Rice noodles
Thi Liên often eats rice noodles, called *pho*, for dinner. She has vegetables with them and either chicken or pork.

Hill fruits
Thi Liên loves eating fruit. The community she lives in grows fruits such as plums, guavas, and bananas.

Sarala from India

Seaside village
Nine-year-old Sarala lives in a village by the sea. She loves the smell of the sea and walking along the beach. Her pet goat is called Amu.

Wearing jewelry
Sarala likes wearing ankle bracelets. She wears arm bracelets as well.

Pink beauty
This colorful plant is called a bougainvillea and grows near to Sarala's house.

Australasia

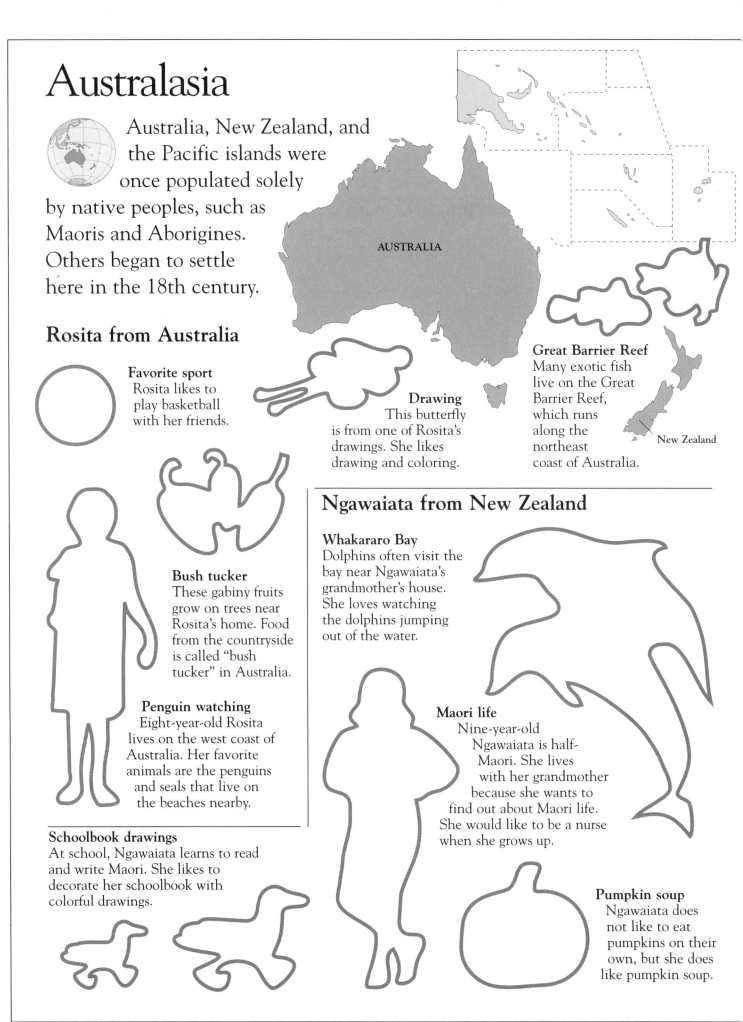

Australia, New Zealand, and the Pacific islands were once populated solely by native peoples, such as Maoris and Aborigines. Others began to settle here in the 18th century.

AUSTRALIA

Rosita from Australia

Favorite sport
Rosita likes to play basketball with her friends.

Drawing
This butterfly is from one of Rosita's drawings. She likes drawing and coloring.

Great Barrier Reef
Many exotic fish live on the Great Barrier Reef, which runs along the northeast coast of Australia.

New Zealand

Bush tucker
These gabiny fruits grow on trees near Rosita's home. Food from the countryside is called "bush tucker" in Australia.

Penguin watching
Eight-year-old Rosita lives on the west coast of Australia. Her favorite animals are the penguins and seals that live on the beaches nearby.

Ngawaiata from New Zealand

Whakararo Bay
Dolphins often visit the bay near Ngawaiata's grandmother's house. She loves watching the dolphins jumping out of the water.

Maori life
Nine-year-old Ngawaiata is half-Maori. She lives with her grandmother because she wants to find out about Maori life. She would like to be a nurse when she grows up.

Schoolbook drawings
At school, Ngawaiata learns to read and write Maori. She likes to decorate her schoolbook with colorful drawings.

Pumpkin soup
Ngawaiata does not like to eat pumpkins on their own, but she does like pumpkin soup.